SEEDS OF MANA'O
Thoughts, Ideas and Opinions
in Poetic Prose

by Branch Isole

SEEDS OF MANA'O
Thoughts, Ideas and Opinions in Poetic Prose
by Branch Isole

Printed in the United States of America

Library of Congress Control Number:
2004101140
ISBN 0-9747692-1-5

Mana'o Publishing
PO Box 1696
Lahaina, HI 96767-1696

My poetry is inspired by the Hula.
The Hula is precise, sensual, sexual
and sophisticatedly raw as it tells a story.
I am a voyeur of the Hula for all its character.

The poems herein are short stories of
issues and emotions surrounding personal
responsibility choice and avoidance.
This is 'Voyeurism Poetry'.

Seeds of Mana'o contains adult material and
language, some cf which is sexual in nature.
It is intended for mature audiences only.

Contents

Introduction

Mana'o (pronounced Ma Na O) is
Hawaiian for 'Thoughts, Ideas and Opinions.'
The Seeds of Mana'o are all around each of us,
in our world and on our paths. Cast on the
winds of universal time and space, waiting for us
to grasp them and make them our own, they are
the seeds of our journey. By watering those that
have been planted in our soul, spirit, mind and
body we each blossom to become who we are.

May the contemporary poems herein,
stimulate your mind and your emotions.
It is truly a pleasure and blessing to be able to
share these *Seeds of Mana'o* with you.
Enjoy the garden.

Branch Isole

I have believed in money
but all I got was greed

I have believed in vengeance
but all I did was bleed

I have believed in fame
but fame turned its back on me

If I had only believed in love
I would have been set free

-Peter Himmelman-
from 'Set Free'
on "Skin"

+ -

Even perfect balance
Requires opposition

A Mother's Love

The one thing we can all learn
From the true love of a mother
Is how to be more considerate
In our treatment of another

Abandoned Never

Lord open my mind
that I might know Your Word
Open my heart
that I might learn Your Ways
Open my eyes
that I might see Your Truth
This,
and every new day

Fill me with Your love
Your simple Commands
That I might now better understand

Not forgetting my past
my sins
my transgressions,
but living anew
with forgiving intentions

You have always been here
Now, that's perfectly clear
It is I who was blind
refusing to see
Spent the time thinking
it was all about me

Fill the void
which lives within me
Mend the break
within my heart
Become one with my conscience again
From this moment,
We start

Apple Core

'She made me do it'
he told the judge
'she was tempted
and then succumbed'

"So she gave right in
without a fight?
That's what you're saying,
Am I hearing you right?"

'That's correct, sir
she knew it a lie
and I think she knew
the whole damn time'

'She said
it wouldn't wash
Not with you sir,
but that didn't
for one minute
stop her'

'No sir,
she was convinced
she could have it all,
then proceeded to shackle me
chain and ball'

"So you tried to refuse
her advances
her wanton ways?"
"For how long was this,
an hour, a day?"

'Ah, to be exact
I don't recall
Remember I mentioned
that chain and ball?'
'I tried to get away
but she was so beguiling
I had to stay'

"So you told her outright
you told her 'No' ?"

'Well, she's a temptress
That's for sure
You know she's all woman
not a little girl'

"My question was
did you tell her 'No'
in no uncertain terms,
Explaining to her
you are both here
new lessons to be learned"

'Oh yes sir!
That was it,
but you know her
a voice like a lair'

"So she dragged you down,
down to the ground?
You resisted, you kicked
you screamed?"

'Yes, that's it,
it was your previous instructions
to her I preened'

"So in summation,
you resisted
you tried
She convinced
she lied?"

'Correct sir
she overwhelmed me with words
It was in the way she acted,
She held it out
I retracted'

"However, you gave in
believing her to be right?
And then,
you,
took a bite?"

'Yes I admit it,
I thought I was free
to do that which I might'

"You listened to her
instead of me
Your actions
I wanted to forgive,
but then when on my walk
I called out,
you hid"

"Why didn't you come out
and admit your transgression,
apologize and explain
you had learned your lesson

Then ask forgiveness
of my redeeming love
Instead of refusing responsibility
and passing the buck"

"For the balance of your life
you shall toil without rest
and as for your efforts
to place blame somewhere else
My sentence upon you,
is death"

At My Door This Week

From our beginning
it was then I knew
as we both talked
only of you
No small place for me
in heart or brain
Against my own will
my emotions did strain

Pulled to and fro
if only I'd known,

but wait,

I did . . .

There beneath the shadows
did truth and reality peek,

Divorce
came to my door this week

Lust filled days
Craven sex soaked nights
You demanded
You demeaned
Slowly at first
yet always from you
a steady stream

I struggled to breathe
both awake
and in dream
My soul clamored
from you to break
My mind and body
wanton slaves
of your honey and cream

Setting a trap for myself
my promises to please
All the while sensing
deep within my being,
muzzles to muffle
the truth that did shriek

Divorce,
came to my door this week

Building a stage
upon which to flaunt
the props you required
until each and every
was fully acquired
Climbing debts' pedestal
with titles desired
It would take my death
from you, to retire

Hooks buried deep
into meaty flesh.
down to the bone
your truths, all lies
Children; assurance, you'd never be alone

A proffered lifetime meal ticket
now punched and paid for

Divorce, this week
came to my door

Baby

I've been missing,
missing my baby
Sometimes her smell
on the pillow
next to me
is enough to start
all those fantasies
The things she does
The things she can
makes me feel
once again
total man

In a world that wants
to keep me down,
down on the ground
to grind and grovel
for a lousy buck
It's she
who keeps me sound
It's she
who remains my luck

That which moves me forward
constantly,
is the loving touch
of my baby

for CC

Bachelor

It started with Nancy
'Golden Shower' girl was she
liked to travel and cruise
the open high seas

Along came Janice
who liked being on top
that sexy girl never wanted to stop
Each time we hit
her tender 'G Spot'
she would go into
orgasmic shock

Balancing her with Carol
was quite a feat
insuring the two of them
never would meet
Carol was
another man's whore
she liked me to use
her back door

Then there was my brother's
mother in law
We met at a motel
in Stanislaus

Did Julie's boss,
her best friend from work
Said she wanted my 'lollipop'
to lick and to slurp

Judy Judy
Judy would do
any and everything
for a good screw

Along came Jill
from up the hill
Like to give hummers
just for the thrill

Reminds me of Mike
yes, that was her name
Did it all with a smile
and never was shamed

Mercy came
came on like a flood
She'd do it anywhere
in water or mud

Peggy and Robbie
wouldn't give head
for them sex was always
'Missionary' in bed

Met sweet Marla
Forty-Two double D
Those at least
I wanted to see

To touch
or suckle
actually, hopefully both
Then squirt on her face
and down her throat

Kathy said she wanted
to start each day
with a little or a lot
of heated foreplay

Carla took me
in her hand
and stroked my ever
enlarging male gland
Licked the tip
to get the last drop,
but never ever
wanted on top
Got on all fours
and looked back with a smile
saying "Come inside big boy
and stay for a while"

Lisa like a rabbit
ready to go
but she never
learned how to blow

Noel was running
from her past
Looking for her future's next
to be her last
Shyly got naked
wouldn't be touched
Then I realized
this girl was touched

Lawyer Linda liked to play golf
Came on vacation to play a round
and have some much needed fun
Took out a club
and her golf ben-wa balls
Hid each and said
"there's still room for you"
Then invited me
to sink a hole in one

Kim never teed a golf ball up
but sure like to do it
on the sixteenth green
right next to the cup

I'd like to take a moment
to thank each of you
And although there have been
more than a few
Most names I've forgotten
having no figment to see
And surely for them
I'm not even a synapse memory
For each of you named
herein today
I'd like you to know
You made me a better person
man
lover,
and you each
helped me grow

So whoever I am
at this point in life
Free from struggle
Free from strife
All failures were mine
and I know through and through
all my success
is in part due to you

Bird Brain

Another 'dog eat dog'
day ahead

Anxieties mixed
with a pinch of fear

Wishing I could
stay right here

Stay cuddled and cozy
all nice and nested
instead of going out
again to be tested

Scratching out a living,
if you could call it that
Pure and simple,
it's survival
Existing on discarded crumbs
while outmaneuvering
all of my rivals

After a long day of tarrying
from pillar to post
and begging your pardon
not to boast,
at each stop
getting the most
from a wide variety
of memorable hosts

It's been said,
'the early bird gets the worm'
and it's true
we all enjoy
seeing them squirm

My question is simple
and here's what it is
Is this what my life
is all about?

Searching for food and flying
and flying, . . .
on the way,
to dying

For my part
I'm ready
just say the word,
but such is the daily
life of a bird

Blessings

Learning early the fear
of discipline
Not from love
but from falling tears
Cowering back from possibilities
Afraid to go forward
stricken for years.

Again and again
opportunity knocked
Still doubt reigned
over actions and talk.

Sacrificed, on the front
Thrown to lions
and bullies in alleys
Young lives strapped and bound
shackled beneath
down in the galleys
To row ever bow-ward
while facing astern
Left to starve,
to rot and to burn.

Where is the grace
the saving face?
Where is the finish of this race?

Living vicariously
through his own seed
Remembering his longings
his failures
his need.
Waiting and waiting
day by day
As time slips slowly
then faster away
Frightened by his future
Running to,
or from his past
Caught between anticipation and regret
Surely, not the last.
Missing the moment
beating himself up
One more time
not nearly enough.

To be led astray
by those loved and trusted
To attempt one's own flight
from being used,
abused
scourged
and busted.

Broken bones, broken homes
History repeating itself
Realizing finally
We each are alone.

Alone on our journey
from there to here
and perhaps,
even back again
Regaining our souls
Released from our sin.

Sins of the world
Sins of mankind
Actions of evil
continue to bind.

To bind us, to threaten us and finally for death
To be released once again for the ultimate test

Living vicariously
through her own seed
Sensing her longings
her failures
her need.
Waiting and waiting
day by day
As time slips slowly
then faster away
Frightened by her future,
Torn by her past
Caught between anticipation and regret
Surely not the last.
Missing the moment
beating herself up
One more time
not nearly enough.

Do we believe?
In whom
what and why?
Believe and smile at our final relief?
Or once more to try,
to cry. . .
and still wonder why?

Each coin has two sides
And so too the sword
So it is with life and death
For believer and non, of God's eternal Word.

Stretched pass the point of no return
this way or that,
to go on
or turn back?
Turn to where?
Which way?
What door?
The world waits and tempts
with its many whores.

Living vicariously
through our own seeds
Knowing our longings
our failures
our needs.
Waiting and waiting
day by day
As time slips slowly
then faster away

Frightened by our future
Tortured by our past
Caught between anticipation and regret
Surely not the last.
Missing the moment
beating ourselves up
One more time
Never enough.

We stumble, we fall
along the route
One moment elated
the next down and out.

Waiting on the meaning
of this bold life
Waiting to excise
with its cold knife.
Feeling the blade
made of steel
Buried deep,
falling to kneel
Cutting out of the heart
all its disease
Cutting out the sins
and finding release.

One life has ended
a new one begun
Finally,
wisdom and freedom to run.

His Blessing now given
and now understood
Not made of
stone
marble
or wood
The Blessing of Life;
Love,
one-hundred proof

The Blessing received
revealed in the Truth.

Blue Tooth Importance

It's obvious
from your Blue Tooth
how important you must be,
to yourself for sure
and quite possibly
to all of creation,
but please
must we all listen
to your inane conversation

Bull's Eye

How Lord
can we possibly
stand before you?

You know
of those things hidden,
veiled within our hearts
The jewels
and precious stones of sin
bedecking our crown
of lusts and cravings
To you suspicions? No
Your awareness is
right on the mark

An arrow already flown
it's perfect placement
suddenly shattered.
its shaft splintered
by one even more precise
following in its path

So exacting is your knowledge of us,
our sinful nature
wishes and desires

There is but one way
for us to have avoided
our unrepentant acts
Thereby being held accountable
for nothing
That would be, not to be;
To have never been born again

Then our loss
would be two fold
First, we would know nothing of you
Then, we would believe ourselves sinless
and in no need
of your redemptive love and compassion

Bush League

They sent us here
a political reaction
Now we're inserted deep
between rival factions

All claim to be
fighting for freedom,
Freedom fighters one and all
their Jihad buzzwords do they extol

The real fight however,
is for crude oil control

It is we who are caught,
caught in the middle
caught between
propaganda and spittle

The entire area
a tempest teapot
Boiling over daily
with religious fanatics
and terrorist plots

It is we who are caught,
caught in the middle
caught between
propaganda and blood's trickle

The entire area
a teapot tempest
Provincial groups all claim
It's only they who know best

It is we
who are caught,
caught in the middle
caught between
propaganda and political drivel

All I know
is the world
hates US more
as we GI's
try to stay alive
and finish out
this last tour

Death's Door Opened

he pulled out the weapon
the smell of fear in the air

one step behind the poor
one step ahead of the dead,
calamity

me,
filled with dread

no time left
to spend or lose,
flashing life

me,
shot dead

preparing for the ultimate trip
the one whereby
i am mortality stripped

left naked,
a wandering soul

anticipating the worst

hoping and praying
for heaven's streets

paved with a love
bright as gold
remembering words once spoken

of reap and of sow

cold words now
no warmth
from mind's hearth glow

yet flames
now
do they rise

burning before

and
behind, tired eyes

flames burning brightly
with the heat
of love?

from above

or the sear of pain
ever to grow

from below

trigger finger twitch
barrel blast
smoke

bullet's blur
entering flesh
upon its path

blackness
distant pinpoint
of light

time tunnel
travel
for my soul

eternity ahead
free from grief

or

forever separated
to join the wailing
and gnashing of teeth

Emotional Expenditures

The cost to the heart
Can be all or nothing,
But the currency of love
Is commitment

Endangered Species

An endangered species
exists in life,
inching closer
each and everyday
becoming soon enough
only a memory,
fading like the setting sun
slowly,
almost imperceptibly
slipping away

Each breath lingers
momentarily
and then,
evaporates invisibly
each, part of a process
whereby all systems
are sustained
by night,
by day

Evading the end
by ignorance
bliss
or denial,
running sadly from
and yet, steadily toward
death's reprisal

The race goes on
the human species too
but for the individual,
for me, for you,
our personal demise
is right on time

Our ends draw near
whether comforted by calm
or clutched by fear,
Whether blessing or curse
your presence here
has altered the course
of the universe

Essentials

Of the many things
men dislike most,
shopping
is one
of which they boast

But alas
a thought
concerning items
sold and bought

Without the essentials
scoured, hunted
and purchased
by wives
and by mothers,
there might be many
unfed, unclothed
and cave dwelling,
husbands
sisters
and brothers

Fear in Black and White

I met Nicole Brown Simpson today.
Not really,
but a woman
just as blonde
just as beautiful . . .
just as frightened,
You could see it in her eyes

On her lap, sat
a stunningly attractive child
Next to her stood,
a rugged Adonis like figure
leering down possessively at her
as he accepted his award
and the adulation
of an adoring, unknowing public

The air between them was palatable
A space once charged with lustful energy
now contained fear
and sparks,
just beneath the surface
of a forced smile with perfect white teeth
and a sinister sideways glance
from dark insecure eyes

What is it that makes these trophies
so endearing, so desired,
yet so dangerous a combination?

It is not black and white
It is something else
Something more base
Something more need filled

It is more.

It is, look at me
I've made it
I've arrived,
I will laugh in the face of convention
The one I long to be part of
and at the same time, beg to defy

The bruises are covered,
masked by make-up
and the finest couture
But fear, still resides there
Behind eyes that see running
and a memory that clings
to the temporary safety
of a locked bathroom door

He said,
"If you ever try to leave
I'll kill you"
and she believes him

So she stays,
Smiling for the cameras
and fearing for her life

Final Flight

What a trip
it's going to be
to leave the body
finally

A soaring spirit
once again
no longer occupant
of a flesh and blood pen

What once seemed
so permanent,
turning to dust
or ash
As essence,
spirit
flies free,
free at last

No longer afraid
frightened
or scared
No longer anxious
of the soul being bared

For each
and everyone
an accounting
will take place
For every living being
of what once was
a human race

All will have a chance
to stand before the assemblage of heaven
Explaining their actions
and responses
without ego, or self inflation,
as if bread
unleavened

And what will you say
on that last judgment day?
Claim ignorance
Misguided perseverance
Complicated resistance
What?. . .
Led astray?

Or willful disobedience
in the belief
you would never have to pay?

God has drawn
a line in time
and only He knows
its reason and rhyme

The Light
of His judgment day,
holds a dark of night
for all who will not
find His Way
before their final flight

Fornication Under Command of the King

I've heard it said
this word among words
came from Jolly Old England
In a time when one
would ne'er against the King
take a stand

Whether by right
or command
or acquiescence to obey
This word has certainly
found its way
into mainstream's vernacular today

Once a word
of action taken
Now an adverb
for extensive use to be making

Hearing it verbalized
again and again
As often as every
second or third utterance
by some women
and many men

Its impact lost
Its intensity no more
What once was reserved
for seaman and whore

Is now heard constantly,
a conversational part
No longer genitally based
It's now tied to the heart

One more instance
of mass desensitizing
Like disrespect and mayhem
in society rising

Conversationally coupled
with two close cousins
we now also hear
mo' and mo'
Two denigrating monikers
ascribed to women,
the female descriptors
'bitch and ho'

For those who use it
No view of love
or lusting
Peppering their immature oral excursions
Proves their superfluous language disgusting

Freedom's Risk

Our postman is
a likeable fellow
his demeanor appears
to be quite mellow
But hidden deep
beneath his affability
and masked behind
his smarmy smile
lurks a sinister
Aryan sieg heil

There are clues
when he speaks
about the things
that he'd teach
to our youngsters
if he could,
to our children
he definitely would

About hate
and terror
and supposed superiority,
about crimes
misdemeanors
and major social felonies

There's no telling
what's in the trunk
of his car
Could be bags
of undelivered mail
and bills
or worse,
weapons
designed to kill

I'm glad my time
with him is limited
to about ten seconds a day
and I wouldn't want to be
another letter carrier
on the day he doesn't
get his way

He's a letter carrier
but he could be,
she
CEO
librarian
or poet's face
and work at the school
local church
grocery store
or some other
unassuming place

For it's not a postal
phenomenon,
but one of the risks
of living in freedom

Freefallin'

Hassles at work
never seem to end
breaking rules
only meant to bend
at 4:55
I hear my callin'
at 5:01,
I'm freefallin'

In the doghouse
because I won't
'Honey Do'
Dinner for me and Rover
bones for two

Sneakin' in
I'm couch bound
Lights off
not a sound
Midnight comes
She's ah stallin'
Once more
I'm freefallin'

Work's a drag
Home's as bad
Weekend's here
time is clear

Poker with the homies
hot roddin' and softballin'
Finally,
I'm Freefallin'

Gentle Breeze

Oh gentle breeze
How long has it been?
How far have you traveled?
The warmth of your being
brushes against my skin,
cooling the radiant air
which surrounds me.

You, oh gentle breeze
whistling through the palms and bamboo
giving voice to those in nature,
those who touch you.

Your life is, as with all God's creatures
small and light in the beginning,
growing in strength and stature
as the day passes.

Becoming at once all powerful
while starting your inevitable decline
into whispered death.

We are born
we grow
and we die.

Only through death
may we experience the opportunity
to live once again.

So it is with you,
So it is with us,
oh gentle breeze.

Hawaiian Sunset

Behold, stretching west
toward Oahu
Blankets of orange and red
Infused with burnished yellow
flaming at its head

Shades of blue layered
by deep nickel cobalt
spreads like frosting atop a cake
Evening's azure sky
prompts our double take
Emerald teal touches
this reef lined beach
Lapping close enough
for us to reach

White sand beaches
Black sand too,
Volcanic red soil
iron rich
through and through

Green forested jungles
bespeckled by rainbow flowers
Blossoms of pink,
fuchsia and purple beckon,
"come closer, sit
beneath my bamboo that towers"

"Oh,
to live in Paradise"
humor tinged sarcasm adds,
"it must be nice"

"Yes, it is"
a bemused reply
"Truly blessed are we
beneath this canopied sky"

"One thing only
makes this sunset
memorably faded
yet never erased,
To share it with you
here in mid-Pacific
as the crescent moon above
slowly gives chase"

(Oahu [pronounced O Ah OO] is the Hawaiian
island where Honolulu is located)

Imaginary Lover

Standing motionless,
Camouflaged
I disappear into the landscape
Watching you
through the small window
as you glide effortlessly around the room
You dance and you tease
Always trying to please
Your imaginary lover,
Who is he?

Seeing you
before the mirror
Enjoying
the both of you
Devouring
your every move
The two of you
under the harvest moon

You dance and you tease
Always trying to please
Your imaginary lover,
Who is she?

You twist and you twirl
Arms in the air
Hands in your hair
Two shy girls
Seductively bare

You dance and you tease
Always trying to please
Your imaginary lover,
Might we become three?

Soon my love soon
Soon will two be
Harmoniously in tune
Two will become one my love,
Soon

You dance and you tease
Always trying to please
Your imaginary lover,
is it me?

Inaccessible

A net of darkness
silently drapes
the back of her neck,
creeping slowly
on its upward trek

Crisscrossing
a defined hairline,
epidermal layer
under muted hue colors
bristle, as if to opine

Energy drains
from lids
and lips
as heaviness settles
upon her hips
Succumbing to labored breathing,
exhaustion induced
and unbridled dreaming

An aura of vibration
more felt than heard
intoned as if by Sirens
to ancient mariners
their words

Glancing quickly
Nothing seen
Oral excitation beckons,
Pressing her
to snap back
into reality

Juxtaposition

His years between twenty and twenty-five
were as hers between five and nine
only,
he was the one who seemed lost

Kingdom of God

Love's eternal presence
On earth, as it is in heaven
is shown
is known
As His sun again rises
each new day, one of seven

The Kingdom of God
Now and forever
Revealed to us
To each who would see
His kingdom
His presence
Always will be

Through His spirit
Flesh made real
That all might hear
His final appeal

Come to Me
Through my Word,
My Son
That you might know how
your race against death
will finally be won,
For your soul to live
not once, but twice
Your salvation
Your redemption
is found in the Christ

Lahaina Town Crier

On the corner he stands
guitar slung,
like an outlaw's gun
First in one hand
and then the other,
the Book

He cries
He hollers
He sings
He laments
Addressing America
His pronouncement,
"Repent"

A neo John
A wilderness voice in paradise lost
Old Testament shame
New Testament cross

Icon tree behind
World around to bludgeon and blunt
Spectators and listeners abound
He,
a commercial affront

Frightened children cry
at his tantrum rant
Adults shriek
against incriminating words
which sting,
as they penetrate the skull
seeking a soft hollow, in each psyche

A knife in the heart
A spear to the lung
Silver bullet to the gut
fired from this,
Gospel hired gun

(Lahaina [pronounced, La High Na] is a town on
the west side of Maui)

Light

The waves crash
upon the rocks
spray, in the air
The tides continue to ebb and flow
always, without a care.

White caps on the horizon's peak
as if flickering off and on
One moment above the surface
the next moment gone.

To gaze out upon its spectrum
spectacle and might
The waters climb and roll
ever changing in their height
Its majesty combined
for my sight
Seeing the small me in perspective
is a thought of awesome fright.

To be lost at sea
no more than a speck
No power or control
to save my neck.

To the depths
do I commit
my mind, my body, my soul
What once was, is, to be no more
That which has always been
free again to soar.

To bob starkly alone
in the dead of night.
Drifting as smoke
lost in flight

Darkness,
despair
loneliness
fright
Waiting for a vision
A sign
A ship
to come
within sight.

Oh to be saved
one way or the other
To be warm and dry
in the arms of another
Reduces the fright,
darkness of night
For from up above
I am seeing a light.

Lucky You

Exactly what sort of miracle
is a birth?
What are the chances
upon this earth,
that you would be born?

Well let's see.
If your mother ovulated
on average
one egg per month
that's twelve or so
in a calendar year.

If she was fertile
for some forty years
you were one in five hundred
of being here.

Pretty good odds
even at that
until you consider
your father was involved
for more than a chat,
and their cooperative
intimate contact
took place,
on only a few select
and particular days.

What was
one in twelve
and grew
to a few hundred
all of a sudden becomes
thirteen thousand, to one

Neither you nor I
have time to toss
that many die,
now throw in this kicker
and you'll better understand
what makes more incalculable
your chance of becoming
woman or man

The pivotal point
of this poem's chant?
For each and every generation
that we count back
exponentially removes you
from your clan's pack

Martyr

Martyrs have something to prove
the questions are,
What?
and to Whom?

Whether misguided by others
or by insecurities
Many feel about themselves
indeed rather poorly

Fighting demons
and ills from the past
They wonder in silence
"How long can this last"?

Why must I allow others
to be so tough?
Why must I continue
to beat myself up?

What release or relief
am I looking for?
That I allow those I love
to knock me to the floor

Will the world like me more
if I cower and bend
Will the ones I wish to please
allow me to make my amends
For the things I haven't done,
except in my head

I know and understand
I'll never be free
as long as I'm unable
to forgive and forget
my acceptance need

Love is not tied
to my need to please,
Except,
It is,
For the martyr who lives
inside of me

Mitochondrial Mybrosis

I know time draws nigh
For circumstances, they mitigate
That is why, I always procrastinate.
Putting off
All of import
Except for a younger
Newer consort.
I could stand straight
Erect and proud
Had I not confided
In so many lies
And wouldn't have fathered
All of this tribe.

Please let me be,
Let me be your friend
I'll be your doormat,
Right up 'til the end.
And when I'm through
Beating myself up
I'll know it was all
Tied to your love.
Use me,
Abuse me
It's okay
Just say you love me
One more time today.

And when you've finally
Used me up
Just tell me
It was my lesson,
In our course
of "Tough Love"

I am the doctor
Or haven't you heard
When I speak,
I proclaim the word.
I am the doctor
Of whom you've heard
Not all have been good
healthy words.
Living large
That's life for me
Only 'one way'
Advancement
If you please.
The youngest
Yea,
That may be so
But I've always known
Which way to go.
So what if I had
to step on those toes
Of books and practice
I've been declaring
My manner,
one of disassociate caring.

The life I've chosen
Woven and weaved
My father, my husband
My nemesis, retrieved.
He said he would
He said he could
But if there was love
It was hidden, denied
veiled in a fog
Thank you lord
For those two dogs.
I know it all
beneath my breath
My reality now
wait for new life,
or death.

Black sheep
Black sheep
Where do you roam?
As the hungry wolf of truth
We beg you,
Stay away from our homes.

Monsters

There's a monster
living under my bed
That's what the one
in the closet said

Old Places

The comfort of old places and old faces
Allows opportunities to slip back
into the old me
Where the sins of my youth
revolt
revel
and run free
In those days
all that mattered was me.

Searching for Truth
Not knowing where to look
Where to sight
Where to see.
Searching the darkness
looking for light
Living in a haze
of hypocritical delight.

Still tempted now and again
Daily, if the truth be told.
Changeable from thought to thought
Testing and questions
which way to go?
The power is within,
be it friend or foe.

Once

Once,
Beauty in women
was Rubenesque
Now it's practiced bulimia
and nervosa anorex

Once,
Concentration camps
made many weak
Now that look is called
'Heroin chic'

Once,
Disfigured or accident victims
relied on plastic surgeon skills
Now it's silicone implants and liposuctions
with which the doctors' days are filled

Once,
Women's lips swelled
from lust filled intentions
Now all it takes
is Botox injections

Once,
Lustrous skin
as ivory or alabaster was adored
Now the desire is tan
Darker than the darkest
laboring field hand

Once,
Pregnancy had a glow,
A glow of new life
for every woman, mother
sister and wife
Now young women
show off their bellies
just to prove they can
Looking like a starving one
from some third world country
or poverty stricken far off land

Once,
A woman's beauty
was accentuated from within
Her sensual appeal
moved countless numbers of men

Have we no shame?
Apparently we don't!
Have we no humility?
Appears we won't!
For now it is all,
all about me
Me
Me

Me
Me
Never about others
or ever about we

The goal today,
push the envelope please
All has changed and spread
throughout today's humanity
Brazen sex and airbrushed vanity
masquerading
as pop culture sanity

One Hand Clapping

Sex alone,
Tentative
Mental fantasies
Bodily response
in sync
perhaps,
maybe,

eventually

Assuming both roles
simultaneously
conversations and thoughts
Finally a rhythm
of hands and genitals

Sustained fever pitch,
mental
psychological
physical

emotionally draining

What started
as a multitude
of extreme efforts
ends quickly,
As if falling from the sky
like a pole vaulter
having missed the benchmark,
waiting for the
sudden impact
of ground,

unfulfilled

Pakanu Road

Driving down the same old lane
make a left onto Pakanu
Each trip imprints new memories
to be added to yesterday's
and all that came before,
wondering what he'll see today

Birthdays?
He remembers the first
from the pictures he's seen
Next to enter his aged mind
good old number nine

Three and four he did know
living in Toronto's cold
with two people
who loved him so,
Grandparents old
yet both young at heart

The ones forgotten
blocked or dismissed
must have meant nothing
on his solo trip

(Pakanu [pronounced, Pa Ka New] is a road in
Haiku [pronounced, High Ee Koo] Maui)

Patrician Prayer

Her spirit has flown
Eternal mystery now shown
The Savior's secret unsealed
His Redemption revealed

No longer alone
one of the world's disposable children
has now gone home

Known once only as words
through her ears were they heard
Alive now
within her soul's heart
Never again, shall she be apart
afar or removed
be it by crack or abyss,
from His love
from His eye
from His voice and caress

Death's design
to drown us
in sin's rising flood
Now crimson cleansed
her soul is saved
by the Lamb's precious blood

The pain
The shame
The world's bestowed guilt
Enough to choke
from heel
to hilt

Her temporal life
now for atoned
by Jesus the Christ
The Christian's way
to God's Holy throne

No longer in need
harm's way
or myopic blur
With open and loving arms
our Lord has received her

Patty now basks
in the light of the Lord
as she sings His praises
with heaven's angelic host
The almighty glories
of Father,
Son,
and Holy Ghost

for Alesha and David

Poetry

Information feeds the mind
Food feeds the body
Poetry feeds the soul

Polynesian Provocateur

Hula,
Where suggestive and provocative hips
meets dirty dancing
in a fusion of cultures
as stories are told with the hands

Rapture

A hard and difficult life
to this place were you led
Troubled souls, tumultuous times
survival mode
constant dread
Culmination of all earthly fears
tested,
in three short years

Exposed to the best
and the worst of us
You, unconditional love
with never a fuss

Offered everything there is
was,
or ever might be
Offered all both man
and the Devil could find
And all you wanted
were the sins and burdens
of all mankind

You could only come once
to set the stage
A triumphant return
in the next age

When shall that be?
Some wait and wonder
when believer and non
will be put asunder
Your words ring true now
as they did then

"In my story
all is shown
Signs, wonders, miracles
by these
they should have known
For those of you here
some intent
some sublime
one day all
will see the sign"

"When this age is over,
and finally done
and into the next
you each finally come
Out of Pisces
and into Aquarius
for it is then
all life shall end
Except for those
whom I call friend"

"My words are clear
for each of you here
Now is the time
to be made aware
of the fortieth day
marked after the event
that fulfilled the role
for which I was sent"

"I mentioned often
for all who have ears
Trust and follow me,
You'll have nothing to fear"

"Heed if you will
all sheep and all goats
My task assigned
to judge every folk
To judge all the same
and deliver into His name,
those who chose to believe
and lived obediently"

"Before the last day
there are decisions to be made
Not only for yourself
but for those whom you love
that none might be lost
but ascend to above"

"It is your choice,
It is up to you,
To know where you'll be
when this age is through"

"Will you now choose
to believe,
and prepare your family
for what lies ahead?

Or ignore God's Word
and continue to be part
of the world's walking dead?"

Skin

Divulging that,
which once meant so much
Exhibited with grandiose regalia
Lapidary birth marks
of independence and new identity

The struggle there-
Selection of graphics and colors
Which,
gazing down
from their linear positions
bejeweling long walls
would be blessed
to be chosen,
Next.

The struggle now-
How to veil and mask
visual distortions
and muted hues
morphing,
on the cavernous convex canvas
As poundage of adipose
is deposited
Settling itself
into its new home

Each nesting bulge
stretching the epidermal murals
and mottled monuments
of mortal markings
on your skin

Soul Bartering

Covetous eyes search left and right
Desires pry into convoluted folds
of meaning and understanding
Rationalizing behaviors
result only in consumption
and so the mercantile wheels turn
spawned by the grease
of credit capitalism
lubricating thoughts of,
More

The call, "buy or sell"
Marketing 101
Supply and demand
Controlling existence for
every woman and man

It has been said
In 'days of yore'
Many succumbed to consumption
Misrepresented colloquially now
as "the big 'C' "
The truth of today's reality;
It's consumption that continues to kill

Death by Debt
Hatched by life's energy
Escalating usury interest rates
Controverted unto the grave

Entrapment? Nay
Not necessary
No need,
Leading the way
Self-indulgence
Sloth and Greed

Charge it
Defer it
Write an I. O. U.
Damn the self-denial cross
God's speed, All ahead full
From morning's wake
until darkness' bed

Irresponsibility
the name-of-our-game
Topped off with a rude coating of
'Have No Shame'

Stewardship

For stewardship examples
to whom can we look?

To what policy
document
paper
or book?

Who can we follow
Who can we know

To guide our responsible service
As your Son always showed

He was from you
surely far above us

To whom can we turn
To whom can we trust?

Give us a common man
one of our own

Who has received your blessing
and represents your throne

That we might know
in some small part

The wisdom that comes
from a discerning heart

Let him show us
how to be strong

Have him teach us
between right and wrong

We are no more than ordinary men
Selfish and ruthless corralled in pens

Pens of our own making
lusts and desires

Pens of our own illusions
with grandiose spires
Reaching to the heavens
we know it all,
just ask us.

His simple reply
"Whoever can be trusted with little,
can be trusted with much."

Sugar Daddy

Jealousy behind darting eyes,
which aisle can she be on now?
There she is!
No . . .
that's not her,
Blonde
but not the loin
he knows intimately
by touch and by heart
its curvaceous line and tone

As the prospector sees the crag of stone
which hides the mother lode
of his fortune
all waking and sleeping hours
So it is with the insecure male
who visualizes,
nay, idolizes
his love and her attentions
awake and in dream

Caught between
mental anguish and angst
an anticipatory act
plays itself out as real
in his head
as he volleys responses
to and fro

What to say, which way to go?
as if propelled
by some unknown hand
prodding him to follow,
stealthily stalking

Even while walking
hand in hand,
his body and mind
strain in agitation
As she merely shops
for lingerie items
which please and piqued
his perceived ownership

Teacher

teacher, teacher
should have been a preacher
talking, talking
balking, gawking,
when we don't know Your answer

force-fed Your favorite subject
charging through Your cherished notes
onward, onward
ever onward
as if You were a Bengal Lancer

we all sit quietly
pencils in hand
each #2 at the ready

Your test before us
Your last command
"get ready, get set, go go go"

moments later
marks and erasures
cover the paper land

salivating without a break
finding each and every mistake,
how smug Your smile
how cyclical Your wit
as Your red pen slashes
in a furious fit

teacher, teacher
have You always been this way?

or is it only since
You've had us
as Your prey

The Cost

"Stifle yourself"
Archie Bunker used to bellow,
wonder if that's what made him so mellow

"Be seen and not heard"
was the cry of the fifties,
wonder if that's what led to the sixties

The millennium comes
now everyone speaks
"I'm the victim here"
they continue to shriek
"I can't be responsible
for actions my own,
just throw me one more
golden bone"

Only one thing
I want to pursue
Just "fifteen minutes"
on Oprah will do

To be a star,
be it Rock
Jock
or TV schlock
It really doesn't matter to me
As long as they
will pay me a fee

"Anything and everything for money"
is my creed
A gilded cage is all I need
Lined with greenbacks, in and out
"I'm the star,
give me my way
or I'll have to pout"

Abstract concepts
Comprehension,
Analysis skills?
I don't do anything
against my will
Read and write?
Watch me whine
It's the mirror's image
for which I pine

It's all about me
not you, not them
certainly, not we
I model my life after MTV

They say
"the world doesn't owe you a living"
I don't care
as long as it keeps giving
the things I want
desire
and covet
I'll start with the monies
of Warren Buffet

What makes you think
I've got it wrong
I'll gladly parade
around in a thong
Or go topless
or bottomless, if you require
Any day,
any night
if you'll pay by the hour

Against the law?
Today the law is for naught
"It's as good as legal
if you don't get caught"
Used to be
breaking the law made it illegal
Not anymore
if you have a legal eagle

'Whore' once was demeaning,
but never no mo
Now women gladly
wear the badge of a 'Ho'

And a man was ashamed
to be known as a dog
His word was his bond
never clouded by 'self' fog
He'd be embarrassed to lie,
steal and cheat
On Main, First and Elm
or even Wall Street

Now he need not
talk the talk
It's always the dollars
that make 'the cock of the walk'

Were we always pristine,
pure
and perfectly white?
No, not really,
man has always used
the absence of light
To perpetuate
and extend his might
As he struggles
in a constant fight

Whether in our world
or in our hearts
our human way
is to live in the dark

No,
things haven't changed
across the ages
Mankind's history
is found on the pages
of eternal struggle
between good and evil

For each must choose
for him or herself
the cost of one's
soul retrieval

The Hoe

the thief loathed himself the need
yet did he love the challenge,
for this reason
he padded with bare feet
when at work

the socialite hated zircon
yet brandished unabashedly silicone,
painted smile upon that face
head full of dreams unknown

Life
Death
all here destined to know
rich
poor
what is it that determines the row
to which we each put our hoe?

Wedding Words

Starting alone
Each on your own
Separate paths in this life
Today you become
Husband and wife

Best friends
And lovers
You've shared
Hardship and fun
Today,
Two become one

Joined together today
For all the world to see
Ones become two
I becomes we

Learning to bend,
Not break
Being real,
Not fake
Truth and commitment
A relationship must
In addition to these
Love, honor and trust

Leaving two pasts behind
One new future ahead
Hand in hand together
Today, two are now wed.

Westside AM PM

Assorted libations
for visitors here
This one Mai Tai
that one cold beer

Limping in
having been baked
a reprieve from old Sol
they wish now to take
Liquids and shade
on their minds
'Please, oh please
with my
shoulders and back
be kind'

Between lobster red
and fuchsia pink burnt
if asked
most answer,
"Oh, it doesn't hurt"
and to prove themselves
stupid,
leave off their shirts

Thank goodness Mom has
common sense about her
and a bottle of
Hana Botanicals
'After Sun Soother'

Battling fatigue
after a morning's beach outing
it's time for a cool one
and Luau scouting

Where to go
What to do
Schedule A, B or C
Wish someone knew

For Dad,
golf and fishing
Mom,
tennis
book by the pool
Teens
surf
snorkel
scuba,
For all shopping
and of course, henna tattoos

And that's,
all before two

At five,
condo rendezvous

Where to go
What to do
Schedule A, B or C
Wish someone knew

Night time,
Ulalena
Gump and Hard Rock Café
Ruth's Chris steak
and a Lappert's shake
Studs and studettes
with whom to flirt
a late night
BJ's Pizzeria
decadent dessert

Where to go
What to do
Schedule A, B or C
Wish someone knew

Tomorrow, same O
same O
all on the go
so many things to do
Anyone for Haleakala biking
if so, be up at two

Sunrise
Sunset
and each hour
in between,
a paradise
of 'E Ticket' rides
for every adventure lover

Only problem incurred
you must return home
just to recover

(Luau [pronounced, LOO OW] is a Hawaiian
feast)

(Ulalena [pronounced, OO LA LAIN AH] is a
live stage production in Lahaina
[pronounced, LA HIGH NA])

(Halekala [pronounced, HA LEE AH KA LAH]
is the East Maui volcano mountain)

What We Say

When we say
"I love you"
what is it we do?
Verbalize an emotion
of something we feel
then begin convincing ourselves,
it's real?

What is real?
The here and now,
This life,
a year, a month, a day
The number of breaths
being exhaled away?

With part of those breaths
we say "I love you"
but isn't love about
less what we say
and more what we do?

Behind these three words
which hold so much
emotional thrust
We say "I love you"
as claimants to overcome
all other things,
solemnly evidenced
by the giving of rings
We know there's lust
but is there trust?

For six months
we're thrilled,
For six more enthralled
For the next twelve
it's still, sort of a ball

About two point five years
of wedded bliss
drops of complacency
begin to exist
Passionate becomes pecks
without so many 'dears'
While intimacy can become
hit or miss

We still say
"I love you"
and do truly believe
After all,
we've made a Commitment
never to leave

The dreaded "C" word
the one we men fear
has taken root
and its head does it rear
So we say,
"I love you"
convincingly enough to get by
as we start to envision
ourselves on the sly

We say
"I love you"
and desire it to be so
hoping it is
and together we'll grow,
instead of apart
our teaming success
not tearing at hearts,
and families
and peers
the ones we've become enmeshed with
through the years

For some who say "I love you"
Theirs is a spiritual connection
A commitment takes hold
where two grow together
solid and bold

For two spiritually growing
in strength as well as length
time becomes blurred
As a life's commitment
begets to serve

Each in love
these two can now see,
understand and behold
when they say
"I love you"
It's better than gold
worn or owned

As two spirits join
becoming a co-nurturing one
Each discovers anew
the eternal joy
in the true meaning of,
"I love you"

You Decide

You want to play
You've got to pay
We all learn that
Life's hard way

We beg, steal and borrow
yesterday, today and tomorrow
And into each life
comes its own sorrow

The trials
the tests
the challenges and quizzes
We all have our times
of self "Gee Whizzes"

Why me, why not him or her or them?
Why is my ice always so thin?

We lie
We try
We always deny
Our mask we present
and continue to cry

Truth? What truth?
Where the hell is your proof
we ask,
claiming a heart's desire to know
and yet,
still the opposite way do we go

Until at last
we realize our past
has left us aghast,
at the 'lots' we have cast

Our choices have brought us to this point in time
Our lives full of rational reasons and rhyme

We lay down at night
full of the dread
at what lies before us
in the new day ahead

Where is the answer?
And how will I know?
Where does my path in the future go?
Will I die in my life?
Or will I grow?
The decisions
The choices
All seeds, mine to sow

Will I learn?
Or finally burn?

The final word
is my own
And surely each day
it is shown
And in the eyes of the mirror
Looking back is what?
understanding . . . . or fear.

Other books by Branch Isole

Barking Geckos ©
Stories and Observations in Poetic Prose
ISBN 0-9747692-2-3

God. . .i believe ©
Simple Steps on the Path of
Spiritual Christianity ™
ISBN 0-9747692-0-7

Order books by Branch Isole at
www.manaopublishing.com
Questions, Comments; go to our website and
click on the 'contact' link.

Living on the island of Maui, Branch Isole is
the 'voyeuristic poet' who shares Mana'o*
and God's Word in writing and with individuals
and groups visiting Hawaii.

Branch also writes poetry, articles and short
stories for journals, magazines, newsletters and
on the Internet at; www.manaopublishing.com

*Mana'o (proncunced Ma Na O) is Hawaiian for
'Thoughts, Ideas and Opinions'.